CORNERSTONE OF FREEDOM

W9-DBH-025

AFRICAN AMERICANS IN THE THIRTEEN COLONIES

BY MICHAEL BURGAN

CHILDREN'S PRESS®
An Imprint of Scholastic Inc.
New York Toronto London Auckland Sydney
Mexico City New Delhi Hong Kong
Danbury, Connecticut

BRINGING HISTORY to LIFE

Scholastic Inc., 557 Broadway, New York, NY 10012.

Content Consultant
James Marten, PhD.
Professor and Chair, History Department
Marquette University
Milwaukee, Wisconsin

Library of Congress Cataloging-in-Publication Data
Burgan, Michael.
   African Americans in the thirteen colonies / by Michael Burgan.
      p. cm.—(Cornerstones of freedom)
   Includes bibliographical references and index.
   ISBN 978-0-531-23600-0 (lib. bdg.) — ISBN 978-0-531-21958-4 (pbk.)
1. African Americans—History—17th century—Juvenile
literature. 2. African Americans—History—18th century—Juvenile
literature. 3. Slavery—United States—History—17th century—Juvenile
literature. 4. Slavery—United States—History—18th century—Juvenile
literature. I. Title.
   E185.18.B87 2013
   973'.0496073—dc23   2012030351

All rights reserved. Published in 2013 by Children's Press, an imprint of
Scholastic Inc.
Printed in China 62

SCHOLASTIC, CHILDREN'S PRESS, CORNERSTONES OF FREEDOM™,
and associated logos are trademarks and/or registered trademarks of
Scholastic Inc.

5 6 7 8 9 10 R 22 21 20 19 18

Photographs © 2013: Alamy Images: 6, 14, 57 top (Everett Collection
Inc.), 5 bottom, 44, 57 bottom (Lebrecht Music and Arts Photo Library);
AP Images: 2, 3, 4 bottom, 4 top, 7, 8, 10, 11, 12, 17, 18, 20, 21, 22, 23, 24,
28, 30, 32, 33, 34, 36, 37, 38, 45, 48, 51 (North Wind Picture Archives), 39
(Osamu Honda), 55 (Paul Beaty); Courtesy of John Carter Brown Library at
Brown University: 5 top, 47; Media Bakery/Kristy-Anne Glubish: cover; The
Colonial Williamsburg Foundation: back cover; The Granger Collection:
40 (John Smibert), 46 (Noel Le Mire after Louis Lepaon), 50, 56 (Susan
Sedgwick), 13, 26; The Image Works: 29 (AAAC/Topham), 42 (Mary Evans
Picture Library), 54 (Topham).

Maps by XNR Productions, Inc.

Did you know that studying history can be fun?

BRING HISTORY TO LIFE by becoming a history investigator. Examine the evidence (primary and secondary source materials); cross-examine the people and witnesses. Take a look at what was happening at the time—but be careful! What happened years ago might suddenly become incredibly interesting and change the way you think!

Contents

Kidnapped

Olaudah Equiano's autobiography is an important source of information for historians who want to know what life was like for enslaved Africans.

Growing up in 18th-century Nigeria, Olaudah Equiano was a happy 11-year-old boy—until he was kidnapped and sold into slavery. Sent to North America, Equiano spent time in the southern colony of Virginia as well

EQUIANO HAD TWO DAUGHTERS,

as farther north, in Pennsylvania. He also sailed with masters on ships that traveled to Europe. Equiano was luckier than most slaves. He had the chance to make money so he could buy his own freedom. As a free man, he educated himself. In 1789, he wrote his life story—the first autobiography written by an American slave.

Most slaves who lived in the colonies, however, are unknown today. If their names were recorded, they were the names their masters gave them, not their African names. Still, some records do exist. From these sources, historians have pieced together how African Americans— most enslaved, but some free—lived before and during the American Revolution (1775-1783).

Slave labor allowed farmers to succeed without paying workers to plant and harvest crops.

JOANNA AND ANNA MARIA.

CHAPTER 1

COMING TO AMERICA

Slaves were captured by fellow Africans and sold to European traders.

WHEN YOUNG OLAUDAH

Equiano found himself enslaved, he already knew something about slave life. Slavery had existed in Africa and other parts of the world for several thousand years. Even Equiano's father owned slaves. Most slaves in Africa had been captured in wars. In some parts of Africa, slaves could work for themselves and own their own slaves. The slave conditions Africans faced in both North and South America were usually much harsher.

Captured Africans were forced to march from their homes to the ships that would take them to European colonies.

Starting in the 1440s, Portuguese traders came to the west coast of Africa in search of gold. But their interests soon changed from gold to slavery. As Portugal, Spain, and other European nations claimed colonies in the Americas, they sought more slaves to grow sugar and other crops in those distant lands. African slave traders captured many slaves far from the coast of Africa and then forced the captives to march to ports, tied together by the neck with pieces of leather. Upon reaching the coast, the slaves boarded European ships.

England competed with other European nations for colonies. These foreign lands were a source of wealth for the rulers of Europe. The first English colony in what became the United States was Virginia. Settlers arrived in 1607 and founded the town of Jamestown. The English came looking for wealth. They didn't find the gold and other valuable minerals they were searching for, but they did begin growing tobacco, which was popular in Europe. Tobacco became an important source of money for the new Virginia Colony.

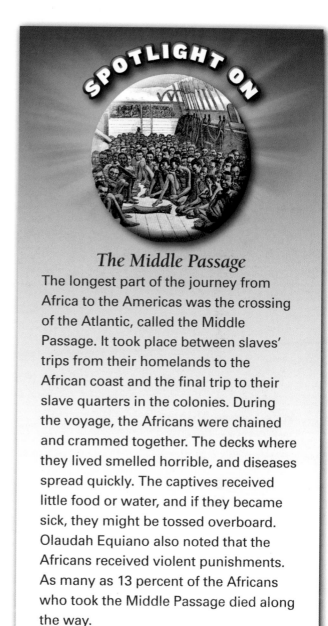

SPOTLIGHT ON

The Middle Passage

The longest part of the journey from Africa to the Americas was the crossing of the Atlantic, called the Middle Passage. It took place between slaves' trips from their homelands to the African coast and the final trip to their slave quarters in the colonies. During the voyage, the Africans were chained and crammed together. The decks where they lived smelled horrible, and diseases spread quickly. The captives received little food or water, and if they became sick, they might be tossed overboard. Olaudah Equiano also noted that the Africans received violent punishments. As many as 13 percent of the Africans who took the Middle Passage died along the way.

In 1619, African slaves reached Jamestown for the first time on record. The colony's leaders traded for them with a Dutch sea captain who had taken them from a Spanish ship. Historians aren't sure if the Virginians considered these 20 or so Africans slaves for life, or just **indentured servants**. This kind of servant agreed to work for a master for a certain number of years and then was freed. Many poor Europeans who couldn't afford to pay their way to America came as indentured servants.

A Slowly Growing Population

Even if these Africans and others who soon followed them to Virginia were enslaved, their lives were different from those of the slaves who came to America during the next century. The children of the first slaves were not always considered slaves, as later children were. No laws kept Africans from marrying white people or owning

At first, some Africans were allowed to own homes and raise families.

property. One African American of the time, Anthony Johnson, owned hundreds of acres of land and had his own servants. Other free African Americans appeared in Virginia through the 1600s. Their lives were similar to those of white colonists. They raised crops and livestock. At times, they traded what they produced for other goods they needed. Some black colonists also had children with white colonists. Their children were called **mulatto**.

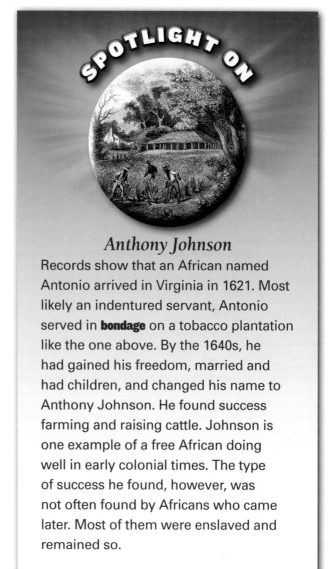

SPOTLIGHT ON

Anthony Johnson

Records show that an African named Antonio arrived in Virginia in 1621. Most likely an indentured servant, Antonio served in **bondage** on a tobacco plantation like the one above. By the 1640s, he had gained his freedom, married and had children, and changed his name to Anthony Johnson. He found success farming and raising cattle. Johnson is one example of a free African doing well in early colonial times. The type of success he found, however, was not often found by Africans who came later. Most of them were enslaved and remained so.

Tobacco plantations spread from Virginia north along the Chesapeake Bay to neighboring Maryland. These two colonies used slaves and indentured servants to raise the crop. Slaves and servants also worked in their masters' homes. Although few laws directly mentioned Africans, they sometimes faced harsher punishments than white people for the same crime. For example, in 1640 one

Slaves were bought and sold as pieces of property.

African servant and two white servants ran away from their masters. When they were caught, the African was forced to remain a servant for life, while the white servants were given lighter sentences.

Laws that limited what African Americans in the Chesapeake region could do began to appear during the 1660s. Virginia ruled that the children of enslaved mothers were also slaves. Both Virginia and Maryland later outlawed marriage between black and white people. A Virginia law from 1667 stated that being baptized as a Christian did not prevent someone from being a slave. In the past, African slaves who were baptized gained their freedom. Then, in 1680, a Virginia law made it illegal for any African American, whether enslaved or free, to own a gun.

By the late 1600s, fewer Europeans wanted to come to America as indentured servants. Since tobacco growers still needed labor for their plantations, they bought more African slaves. The number of Africans in the Chesapeake region was growing rapidly by the end of the 17th century.

First Africans in the North

In the race to claim American colonies, the Dutch explored land in 1609 that they called New Netherland. (The English would later take control of it and rename it New York.)

Starting in 1624, the Dutch brought African slaves from their colonies in the West Indies to New Netherland. These slaves helped build roads and clear land on the island of Manhattan, which is now the heart of New York City. Some slaves received what was called half-freedom. They were given land and lived outside the Dutch settlement, though they had to pay a tax every year.

Africans also came to the Dutch colony as indentured servants and later lived as **freemen**. The free Africans had legal rights, and at least two won court battles that forced white colonists to pay them money they were owed. Africans could also marry each other in the major Dutch church. When wars with neighboring native groups arose, Dutch officials armed the Africans so they could help defend the settlement.

Dutch control extended over parts of what are now New Jersey and Delaware, so Dutch ships brought Africans to those colonies, too. Later, more African slaves reached New Jersey when the English took control there. The wealthy men who controlled New Jersey offered white landowners more land if they bought slaves, knowing how important slave labor would be to help the colony grow. To the west of New Jersey, the English founded the colony of Pennsylvania in 1681. The colonists soon bought Africans to help clear land and build homes. In these English **Middle Colonies**, Africans had fewer rights than when the Dutch controlled much of the region.

New England Slavery

To the north of New York, English settlers known as Puritans and Pilgrims dominated New England. They had come in part because their religions were not always welcome in England. But the settlers also wanted to make money, so they sought the labor of African slaves. Some African slaves reached Massachusetts in 1638, though records note the presence of several other Africans in that area before them. They were likely indentured servants.

In 1641, Massachusetts became the first English colony in North America to legally recognize the practice of slavery. Three years later, some Massachusetts merchants sent a ship to Africa to buy more slaves. In general, though, the first African slaves in this region came through the West Indies, often arriving on ships that primarily carried other goods between those islands and New England.

Except for Rhode Island, the New England colonies did not have large plantations. Slaves were mostly found in coastal towns and lived with their masters. They often worked as servants in the houses of wealthy families or as artisans with a particular skill. Through the 1600s, Africans were rare in New England. But during the next century, the number of Africans there and throughout the colonies would grow.

Some slaves worked indoors as house servants instead of laboring in fields.

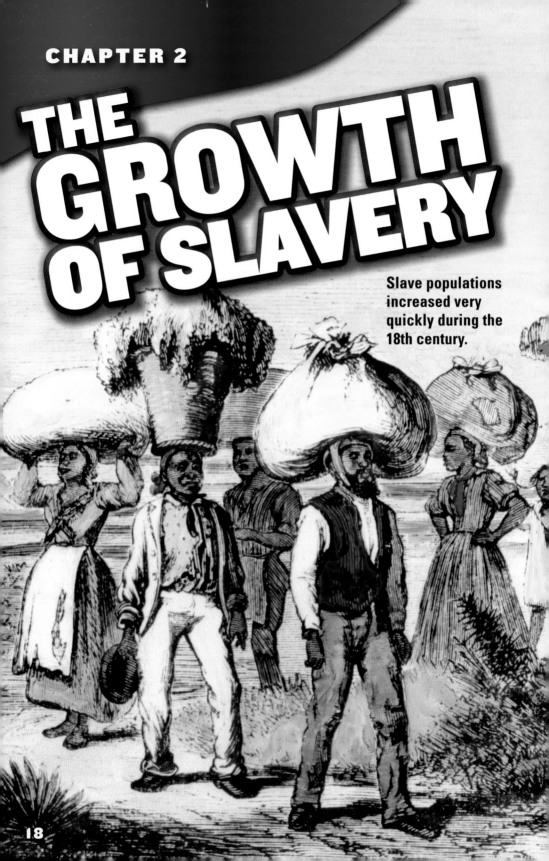

CHAPTER 2

THE GROWTH OF SLAVERY

Slave populations increased very quickly during the 18th century.

BY THE EARLY 18TH CENTURY, Chesapeake landowners were buying more slaves, and Virginia developed the largest African population in the colonies. By 1750, more than 100,000 African Americans lived there, out of a total population of 230,000 people in the colony. Through the 18th century, slavery also grew tremendously farther south. In South Carolina, black slaves outnumbered white colonists.

Some slaves were responsible for cooking and preparing food.

Meanwhile, the number of slaves grew in parts of the North as well, with New York and New Jersey having the most slaves in the region. Still, the number of slaves in the Middle Colonies and New England remained small compared to the South. Parts of those northern regions had more freemen living there than in the South, especially after 1750. Slaves sometimes bought their own freedom, and in some cases they earned more money to buy the freedom of relatives. Some masters left instructions in their wills to free their slaves. Other slaves simply ran away and managed to escape capture.

Rise of Slavery in the Low Country

The English began settling the Low Country, what became North Carolina and South Carolina, during the 1660s and 1670s. The settlers were English planters who had run large plantations in the West Indies using slave labor. They sought to do the same in America. Later, after Georgia—the last of the 13 English colonies—was founded in 1732, slavery arrived there as well.

Both Georgia and South Carolina had warm, swampy conditions along their coasts that were perfect for growing rice. African slaves had experience growing rice from their lives in Africa, so they often made better workers than Europeans did. Rice plantations worked by large numbers of African slaves dotted the coasts of both colonies.

Rice was an important crop in Georgia and the Carolinas.

Slave Markets

Slave markets showed what white colonists thought of enslaved Africans. Slave traders often kept the slaves in jails before bringing them to market, where several hundred slaves might be sold at one time. To owners, slaves were simply property—but valuable property because they provided so much labor. Buyers looked over their purchases carefully, trying to avoid slaves who might have diseases or physical problems. Slave markets were found in both the North and the South. At times, Africans were sold right at the docks where slave ships arrived. Importing slaves into the United States was legal until 1808.

Many slaves came to the region through Charleston, South Carolina, which had a large slave market. Some 94,000 slaves were sold there between 1706 and 1776. The colonies in the South became what some historians call slave societies. The presence of many enslaved Africans shaped the **economy** and culture of the region.

In general, across the South the wealthiest planters owned the most slaves. Small farmers might own one or two at most, and many owned none. Across the colonies, only about 25 percent of white colonists owned slaves. As slavery increased in the South, the number of free Africans fell. By the American Revolution, only about 5 percent of the African Americans in the Chesapeake region and North Carolina were free.

Some families owned just one or two slaves to help with housework.

Northern Slavery in the 18th Century

As in earlier times, northerners who owned slaves in the 18th century often had only two or three. Slaves usually worked on smaller farms or in the household. One exception was in Rhode Island, where several families owned dozens of slaves to run plantations like the ones in the South. In part of that colony, as many as one-third of the workers were African American slaves.

Slavery was also fairly common in the cities of the northern colonies. Boston, Massachusetts, and Philadelphia, Pennsylvania, had large slave populations. So did New York City. The slave population received a boost during the 1750s, as wars between native groups, colonists, and European powers kept European immigrants from coming to America. Northerners turned to slaves brought directly from Africa to provide needed labor.

Life for freemen in the North could be difficult. They faced **discrimination** in finding jobs. Black colonists who owned shops often could not receive the credit they needed to buy goods.

Wealthy people were especially likely to own slaves.

More Limits on Slaves

The growth in the number of African slaves led to more laws affecting black Americans, both enslaved and free. The laws, in part, reflected a growing sense of racism—the idea that Africans, because of their darker skin and different cultures, were inferior to white people. The laws also stemmed from a fear of slave rebellions. Masters knew that all slaves wanted their freedom and that some slaves would fight for it, if they had a chance.

A VIEW FROM ABROAD

While the British counted on slave labor in their colonies, many fewer African slaves lived in Great Britain than in the U.S. colonies. According to William Blackstone, one of the great British legal thinkers of the 18th century, slavery should not exist in Great Britain at all. In the 1760s, Blackstone wrote:

This spirit of liberty is so deeply implanted in our constitution, and rooted even in our very soil, that a slave or a negro, the moment he lands in England, falls under the protection of the laws, and with regard to all natural rights becomes eo instanti [instantly] a freeman.

In 1705, Virginia pulled together a series of laws, called a slave code, that other colonies copied. The code spelled out that slaves were property and that masters had a right to punish slaves who disobeyed them. Punishment could include killing the slaves. A slave could not leave

Slaves risked harsh punishment if they were caught running away.

a master's home without written permission, and slaves could be whipped for breaking even minor laws.

Virginia took away the right of free Africans or mulattoes to vote in 1723 and passed laws that made it harder for masters to free their slaves. The drive to limit rights for African Americans and to make it harder to free slaves took place in the North as well. In New York, for example, a law in 1712 made it illegal for free African Americans to own property. New York and other northern colonies also required masters to pay the government if they wanted to free a slave. The money would pay for freemen who couldn't support themselves. Requiring that fee made masters less likely to free their slaves.

Fighting Back Against Slavery

Slaves, especially new arrivals from Africa, sometimes tried to run away. If caught, they were dragged back to their masters, where they faced punishment. Slaves who didn't try to run away might resist their situation in other ways. Working as slowly as possible or pretending to be sick denied masters their labor. One Virginia planter complained that his slaves "seem to be quite dead hearted and either cannot or will not work."

Some slaves took more active steps against their masters. These slaves set fields on fire or stole livestock,

A FIRSTHAND LOOK AT

ADS SEARCHING FOR RUNAWAYS

Newspapers often ran ads placed by masters seeking their runaway slaves and sometimes their indentured servants. The ads described what the slaves looked like and sometimes what skills they possessed, such as being a shoemaker or sailor. The University of Virginia has a collection of several thousand of these ads just from colonial Virginia. See page 60 for a link to view them online.

which they then sold. A few slaves even tried to kill a master with poison. The most organized way to fight back was for slaves to rebel as a group, but this wasn't easy. Laws prevented slaves from having guns or even meeting with one another beyond their masters' watchful eyes. Yet some slaves did rebel.

The largest colonial slave rebellion took place near the Stono River in South Carolina, in 1739. An Angolan slave named Jemmy led other slaves as they marched carrying a sign that demanded liberty. The slaves had stolen guns, and they began to attack white residents, killing about

Some slaves escaped on horses stolen from their masters' stables.

Runaway slaves were hunted down violently.

20 people. A local **militia** finally killed or captured the rebels. Most of the prisoners were executed. The white residents of the area rewarded some slaves who helped their masters escape the violence. These slaves received new clothes and money. The white colonists wanted to show the slaves that loyalty would be rewarded while attempts to rebel would be punished. So, while some African Americans in colonial America might find freedom through one way or another, most faced a life of bondage.

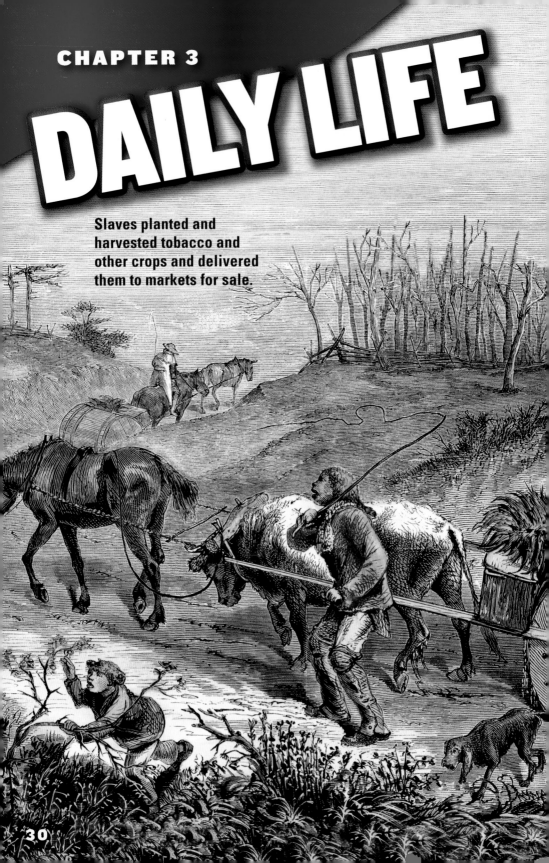

CHAPTER 3

DAILY LIFE

Slaves planted and harvested tobacco and other crops and delivered them to markets for sale.

WHERE AFRICAN AMERICANS

lived, and whether they were enslaved or free, shaped how they spent their days. Like most white Americans at the time, African Americans usually lived and worked on a farm.

In the Chesapeake region, growing tobacco filled 11 months of a slave's typical year. Besides raising tobacco or other main crops, slaves also did chores required to keep a farm running. The work went on all day long, or as slaves described it, from "can see to can't see," meaning from sunrise to sunset. During the 18th century, wheat replaced tobacco as a key crop in the region. Raising grains and other crops was not as backbreaking as raising tobacco, but the slaves still spent long hours in the fields. Children as young as three had some work to do, and by age seven they might spend half a day in the fields and then do other chores.

Slaves often used their days off to spend time with family and friends.

Most planters gave their slaves Sunday off, and the slaves often used the time to raise crops for themselves. But household servants or city slaves sometimes did not get this day off. They were usually under the more direct control of their masters. But compared to plantation slaves, those who worked in cities usually had easier living conditions.

Slaves in the Low Country

On the rice plantations of the Low Country and Georgia, life was especially hard. The slaves had to clear trees and prepare the fields where the rice grew. They then spent long days standing in the watery fields to raise and harvest the crop. Heat and disease killed many slaves. Most slaves on rice plantations were given a specific task to do each day. Planters often hired white men, called overseers, to make sure the slaves did as they were told.

Along with rice, African slaves in the Deep South raised their owners' cattle and grains, as well as livestock and crops for their own food. In South Carolina, indigo became another important crop raised by slaves. The plant was used to make a blue dye. North Carolina slaves

Slaves were forced to work long days doing difficult jobs on rice plantations.

often worked cutting trees for lumber or producing materials, such as tar, that were used to build ships. As in earlier times, skilled slaves might work as carpenters or blacksmiths, and their masters might have them work for other white colonists as a way to make money for the master. Landowners with only one or two slaves worked with them to raise crops.

On the large plantations of the Low Country and other parts of the South, slaves lived in small homes of their own, often with dirt floors and **thatched** roofs. Many slaves had lived in similar homes back in Africa. The homes often had cellars belowground where crops

Slaves lived in very simple homes.

were stored. **Archaeologists** digging at former colonial slave quarters have found artifacts that belonged to the resident slaves. These include such things as tobacco pipes, forks and spoons, and clay pots.

African Culture in America

Living and working mostly away from white colonists, Low Country slaves kept their African cultures longer than slaves in the North or the Chesapeake region. Historians point out that slaves came from a wide area in Africa, so they had different beliefs and customs, as well as different languages. But some parts of life were similar across western Africa. Slaves created a new culture that blended the different African roots with parts of American culture.

The slave culture included dancing and playing music on drums and other instruments also found in Africa. Africans also learned to play European instruments, such as the fiddle. Olaudah Equiano wrote that Africans in America "are almost a nation of dancers, musicians, and poets." The banjo is one African instrument that crossed the Atlantic. To white colonists, African drums seemed threatening, since Africans could use them to send messages. The drums were outlawed in several colonies.

Africans also brought foods with them to America, including okra and yams. Stews that combined many ingredients were popular, as they could cook slowly during the day while the slaves worked. Africans learned about native crops from Native Americans. For a time, white settlers had enslaved some Native Americans, so

African American weddings became more common as time went on.

native people knew the hardships that African slaves faced. Native and African Americans across the colonies often spent time together, sometimes marrying each other.

In the early years of American slavery, white settlers mostly bought African men, since men were stronger than women and could do heavier work. The women who were enslaved were expected to work as long as the men, even if they were pregnant. Because there were so few African women in America in the early years, and laws restricted marriage between white and black Americans, African American men could not start families. During the 18th century, however, slave owners bought more African women. The children of these women also became slaves. Slave families, however, could not be sure that a master would always keep them together.

Religion

Africans who lived separately from white colonists, as was common on large plantations, tried to keep their old religious beliefs alive. Beliefs, just like languages, differed depending on what part of Africa the people came from. A few Africans had Christian or Muslim beliefs. Most accepted western African teachings that said the world was created by one supreme god, though other gods existed. These gods played a role in controlling nature and the world of human affairs. **Ancestors** were thought to help the living by dealing with these gods. Archaeologists have found items, such as small coins, that slaves used in their religious practices.

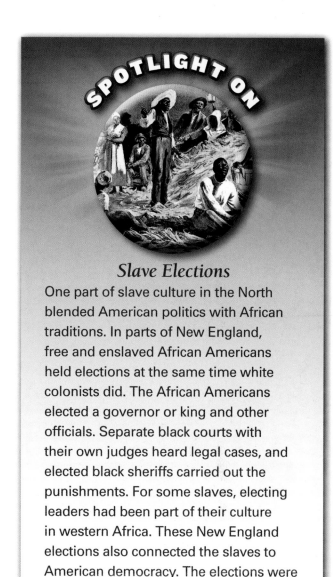

SPOTLIGHT ON

Slave Elections

One part of slave culture in the North blended American politics with African traditions. In parts of New England, free and enslaved African Americans held elections at the same time white colonists did. The African Americans elected a governor or king and other officials. Separate black courts with their own judges heard legal cases, and elected black sheriffs carried out the punishments. For some slaves, electing leaders had been part of their culture in western Africa. These New England elections also connected the slaves to American democracy. The elections were a cause for celebration, often marked by a parade, dancing, and eating.

A FIRSTHAND LOOK AT
AN AFRICAN BURIAL GROUND

On plantations and in towns, African Americans were buried separately from white settlers. One colonial burial ground for African Americans was uncovered in New York City in 1991. By removing the bodies and studying the bones and items that were discovered, historians have learned more about colonial slave life in the city. See page 60 for a link to watch a video about the burial ground online.

Thousands of Africans became Christians after reaching America. New Englanders and the Quakers of Pennsylvania tried to spread Christian teachings to African Americans. Some black children went to religious schools to learn how to read and write. In the South, masters were not always eager to see African

Many African Americans converted to Christianity during the Great Awakening.

slaves become Christians. They did not want them to find out that the Bible talks about the Jews of ancient Israel being slaves and then winning their freedom. Masters didn't want their slaves to seek freedom. Most southern masters also didn't want their slaves to read and write because slaves could use those skills to organize rebellions.

A religious movement during the 1730s and 1740s called the Great Awakening brought Christianity to more African Americans. The ministers in this movement wanted to spread God's word to everyone. They eagerly baptized slaves, but in general they did not speak out against slavery.

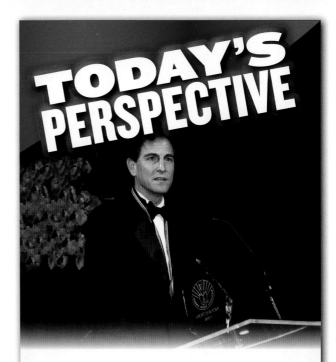

TODAY'S PERSPECTIVE

In recent decades, historians have tried to take a closer look at the relationships between white and black colonists. In cities, poorer white and black people often worked and spent time together. At the large religious gatherings of the Great Awakening, they prayed together. Sometimes, black and white people had children together. In 1998, author Edward Ball (above) wrote about the slaves once owned by his family in South Carolina. He found that several ancestors seemed to have loving relationships with their slaves. But the reality remains: slavery was based on oppression and denied African Americans basic human rights.

CHAPTER 4

REVOLUTION AND FREEDOM

Judge Samuel Sewall was one of the first white colonists to speak out against the unfair treatment of African Americans.

EVEN AS SLAVERY GREW IN THE colonies during the 1700s, some white colonists began to speak out against how Africans were treated. One of the first was Samuel Sewall, a judge in Boston. In 1700, he began a battle with a master who had broken a promise to free an African slave. Sewall wrote that Africans, like white colonists, were children of God and "ought to be treated with respect." Sewall, though, did not think all slaves should be free. He still had some of the racist attitudes common at the time.

Lucretia Mott, the wife of a Quaker minister, was a strong supporter of abolition.

Over the decades, other white colonists spoke more forcefully against slavery. They said enslaving Africans—or anyone—was not a Christian practice. Other white colonists, however, argued that parts of the Bible could be interpreted as supporting slavery.

As a group, the Quakers of Philadelphia began to take the lead in speaking out against slavery. Although the first Quakers in America owned slaves, by the 1750s more Quakers began to feel that enslaving people went against their belief that all people are equal. Some Quakers called for the total **abolition** of slavery.

The Road to Revolution

The call for freeing enslaved African Americans grew as the colonies drew closer to war with Great Britain. In 1763, the British took control of France's former lands in North America. To pay for soldiers and forts to defend all its colonies there, the British wanted the colonists to pay higher taxes. The colonists resisted. Many of them said they did not have anyone to represent their views in Parliament. As the 1760s went on, some colonists protested the new taxes, and the British sent troops to Boston to keep the peace there.

A mulatto colonist named Crispus Attucks played a part in an early conflict between the colonists and the British. He was one of five people killed in 1770, when British troops fired on Boston residents who were threatening the soldiers. The killings became known as the Boston Massacre. Three years later, colonists threw crates of tea into Boston Harbor to protest a tax on tea. The British clamped down on Boston and the rest of Massachusetts. They sent more troops and took away the colonists' rights to run their own government. Soon, other colonies joined Massachusetts in protesting those measures.

During the years of increasing conflict, some Americans accused the British of treating them like slaves. The colonists wanted their freedom, which they called a natural right. African Americans said that they had been arguing against slavery and seeking freedom for years. If freedom was good for white colonists, it should be good for them, too.

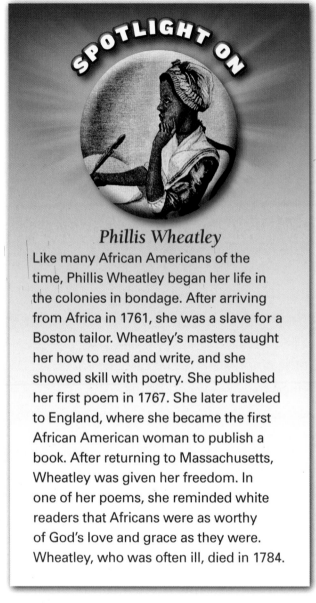

Phillis Wheatley

Like many African Americans of the time, Phillis Wheatley began her life in the colonies in bondage. After arriving from Africa in 1761, she was a slave for a Boston tailor. Wheatley's masters taught her how to read and write, and she showed skill with poetry. She published her first poem in 1767. She later traveled to England, where she became the first African American woman to publish a book. After returning to Massachusetts, Wheatley was given her freedom. In one of her poems, she reminded white readers that Africans were as worthy of God's love and grace as they were. Wheatley, who was often ill, died in 1784.

In 1773, a group of slaves sent a **petition** to the governor of Massachusetts. In it, they asked for their freedom, noting that they had "common with all other men a natural . . . right to that freedom which the Great Parent of the Universe [God] hath bestowed [given] equally on all mankind." Some white colonists saw that their arguments for natural rights and freedom should apply to blacks, too. Abigail Adams was married to John Adams, one of the leaders of the Massachusetts Patriots. She wrote to him that African Americans "have as good a right to freedom as we have."

The War Begins

On April 19, 1775, the American Revolution began. The first battles took place in the Massachusetts towns of

Lexington and Concord, and African Americans fought for the Patriot cause. Prince Estabrook, a slave from Lexington, was wounded on that first day of the war. He would later serve at other major battles during the revolution and earn his freedom. Peter Salem also fought after receiving his freedom from his masters. Other free African Americans, some of whom had been born to free parents in New England, later joined the cause. Lemuel Haynes was a mulatto freeman who fought and later became the first African American minister to work in white Protestant churches.

As the war went on, African Americans served as both soldiers and sailors. As many as 5,000 African Americans fought for the Patriot cause. Some of them were already

Many African Americans served in the Revolutionary War.

African American soldiers fought alongside Revolutionary War leaders such as the Marquis de Lafayette.

free when they entered the military. Others were given their freedom if they agreed to fight, or they were promised it after they served. The southern colonies were less likely to seek African Americans for their military units, though Virginia and Maryland did allow freemen to serve, and slaves could serve in Maryland with their masters' permission. James Madison, who later wrote the U.S. Constitution, believed that some Virginia slaves should be freed and put into the military, but the state's slave owners opposed this. The Virginia government actually bought slaves during the war, to provide labor needed to supply the troops. Leading Virginia Patriots such as George Washington and Thomas Jefferson also owned slaves.

The British employed some African Americans during the war, though not in large numbers. Lord Dunmore, the British governor of Virginia, offered to free any slaves or indentured servants who joined the British cause. Hundreds of African Americans volunteered, but few saw battle. By 1779, the main fighting of the war had shifted to the South. The British offered to let slaves pursue any job they chose if they left their Patriot masters. The British also said that any African American Patriot captured in battle would be sold into slavery.

Thousands of slaves attempted to join the British

YESTERDAY'S HEADLINES

DIALOGUE

CONCERNING THE

SLAVERY

OF THE

AFRICANS;

Shewing it to be the *Duty* and *Interest* of the *American* States to emancipate all their *African* Slaves.

WITH AN

ADDRESS to the owners of such SLAVES.

DEDICATED TO THE HONOURABLE THE

Some colonial writers published short articles called pamphlets. In 1776, Rhode Island minister Samuel Hopkins published a pamphlet called *A Dialogue Concerning the Slavery of the Africans*, shown above. He wrote:

> They [African slaves] see the slavery [that] the Americans dread as worse than death is lighter than a feather compared to their heavy doom...And when they observe all this cry and struggle for liberty . . . and behold the sons of liberty . . . tyrannizing over many thousands of poor blacks, who have as good a claim to liberty as themselves, they are shocked with the glaring inconsistency and wonder they themselves do not see it.

A monument to African Americans who fought during the Revolutionary War stands today at Valley Forge, Pennsylvania.

side even without the offer to work as they chose. In general, slaves of the South believed they would receive better treatment in the future under British rule. Even in the North, some Africans preferred the British to their American masters. In New York, African American boys as young as 11 years old joined the British side, serving as drummers. The military on both sides used the drums to signal their soldiers.

The African Americans who joined the Patriot cause were a key part of the battle for American independence. Along with fighting on the battlefield, they provided important labor for the war effort. Some also served as messengers, and a few were spies. One of these

Slaves were not often depicted in colonial paintings, but James Armistead appears in one with the Marquis de Lafayette, a French officer who fought for the Patriots. Lafayette helped Armistead win his freedom after the war.

slave spies was James Armistead of Virginia. Armistead convinced a British general he would spy for him against the Americans. Actually, Armistead just wanted to get into the British camp so he could gather information for the Americans. For his bravery, Armistead was later granted his freedom.

Victory in War and in Court

In 1781, American forces, with help from France, defeated a British army in Yorktown, Virginia. The loss convinced the British that the war was no longer worth fighting. The two sides soon met to discuss peace—a peace that would grant the Americans their independence.

Before a peace treaty was signed, African Americans were winning their first legal battle to end slavery. In 1781, a Massachusetts slave named Mumbet took her master to court to try to win her freedom. By one report, she was inspired to act after hearing a reading of the Declaration of Independence. In New England, other slaves had won court cases that granted them their freedom. But the decision in Mumbet's case was different.

The year before, Massachusetts had written its first constitution. The lawyer for Mumbet and another slave argued that slavery violated the constitution, which said "all men are born free and equal." The court agreed. A short while later, other courts in Massachusetts did the same in several trials involving Quock Walker, a slave who said his former master had promised him his freedom.

These legal decisions ended slavery in Massachusetts just as the United States was officially becoming a new nation. Slowly, other northern states ended slavery,

Mumbet was also known as Elizabeth Freeman.

An attack on Fort Sumter in South Carolina was the start of the Civil War.

though in most cases slaves had to wait a number of years to be free. The struggle to end slavery across the United States would grow during the 19th century. Many southerners opposed efforts to stop its spread into new states. Some abolitionists wanted it outlawed everywhere as soon as possible. It took the Civil War (1861–1865) to settle the issue. When several states in the South tried to leave the Union to protect their right to own slaves, President Abraham Lincoln said they did not have a legal right to leave. Lincoln did not start the war to abolish slavery, but when the war ended in 1865, the country was in the process of making slavery illegal forever.

What Happened Where?

New York City, New York

Africans had more rights under Dutch rule here, though most Africans were still slaves. Slavery grew in New York City after the English took over. It was the site of a slave rebellion in 1712, and fears of another one in 1741 led government officials to kill 30 African Americans. Dozens more potential rebels were ordered out of the city.

Philadelphia, Pennsylvania

Although the Quakers bought slaves when they first settled in Philadelphia, by the mid-18th century, some Quakers in the city were leading the fight to abolish slavery. One of the most vocal was educator Anthony Benezet, who helped start a school for Philadelphia's freemen.

Charleston, South Carolina

During most of the 18th century the capital of South Carolina was a major port for ships carrying African slaves to the colonies.

GA

BRITISH
NORTH
AMERICA

part of
MA

NH

NY

MA

CT

RI

PA

New York

Philadelphia

NJ

MD   DE

VA

Jamestown

NC

Charleston

Boston

ATLANTIC
OCEAN

Boston, Massachusetts
Slaves and free Africans from the Boston area played a part in early battles of the American Revolution. In 1780, lawmakers in Boston approved a state constitution that helped Massachusetts slaves win their freedom.

Rhode Island
The smallest colony was big on slavery—a law passed in 1652 made slavery illegal, but citizens ignored it. The trade in slaves dominated Rhode Island's economy for most of the 18th century.

Jamestown, Virginia
In 1619, a group of about 20 Africans were sold to English colonists in Jamestown.

N
W   E
S

0   150   300 mi
0   150   300 km

13 Colonies

A Slow Victory

Civil rights leaders such as Martin Luther King Jr. helped fight against the unfair treatment of African Americans.

The end of slavery did not mean the end of difficult times for African Americans. The U.S. Constitution was **amended** to protect the rights of the new freemen, but those rights were often still denied. Not until the 1960s did African Americans see changes in the laws that guaranteed their right to vote. They also continued to face racism and discrimination, especially in the South.

PRESIDENT BARACK OBAMA WON

With the slow improvement of legal rights came new research into African American history. Some of the most important historical work about African Americans in colonial times began during the 1960s. That work continues today.

In 2008, U.S. voters elected Barack Obama president of the United States. Obama's father was born in Africa, and his family never experienced slavery. But just by being African American, the younger Obama experienced racism. His election was a major milestone on the road away from the discrimination that African slaves and free African Americans faced in colonial times.

Barack Obama has made history as the first African American U.S. president.

THE 2009 NOBEL PEACE PRIZE.

INFLUENTIAL INDIVIDUALS

Elizabeth "Mumbet" Freeman

Anthony Johnson (?–1670) came to Virginia as an indentured servant. After finishing his time as a servant, he became one of the wealthiest free Africans of the 17th century.

Crispus Attucks (ca. 1723–1770), the son of a black father and Native American mother, was a runaway slave who settled in Boston. He was killed during the Boston Massacre of 1770.

Prince Estabrook (1740–1830) was a Massachusetts slave who was wounded fighting for the Patriots on the first day of the American Revolution. He later fought in many other battles.

Elizabeth "Mumbet" Freeman (ca. 1742–1829) was a slave in western Massachusetts. She won a court case in 1781 that freed her and helped end slavery throughout Massachusetts.

Abigail Adams (1744–1818) was the wife of Patriot leader John Adams. She wrote to her husband that African Americans deserved the same freedoms as whites.

Olaudah Equiano (ca. 1745–1797) was a slave who bought his own freedom. He educated himself and was the first former slave in America to write an autobiography.

James Armistead (ca. 1748–1830) was the slave of a Virginia Patriot. He spied on the British during the American Revolution, giving George Washington's army useful information.

Olaudah Equiano

Lemuel Haynes (1753–1833) was a free African at the time of the revolution who fought for the Patriots. He later became a minister and served in several white churches.

Phillis Wheatley (ca. 1753–1784) was taken from Africa to America as a slave when she was a young girl. She was educated by her Boston master. She impressed people in both America and Europe with her skills as a poet.

Phillis Wheatley

TIMELINE

1440s

Portuguese traders begin buying slaves in West Africa.

1607

English settlers found Jamestown, Virginia.

1619

Jamestown residents buy about 20 Africans from Dutch traders.

1660s

Planters begin bringing slaves to South Carolina. African Americans eventually outnumber white colonists there.

1680

Virginia prohibits any African from owning a gun.

1700

Samuel Sewall of Boston writes against slavery.

1739

The largest slave rebellion in colonial America takes place in South Carolina.

1770

Crispus Attucks is killed during the Boston Massacre.

1775

The British encourage southern slaves to leave their Patriot masters, and hundreds of slaves do so.

1624

Dutch colonists bring the first enslaved Africans to New Netherland.

1641

Massachusetts becomes the first English colony in North America to legally protect slavery.

1644

Massachusetts merchants send a ship to Africa to buy slaves.

1705

Virginia creates the first slave code, a series of laws that strictly limit the activities of slaves.

1712

New York passes a law barring free Africans from owning property.

1723

Virginia outlaws voting for African and mulatto freemen.

1781

A Massachusetts slave named Mumbet wins a court case that says slavery is not allowed under the state's constitution.

1991

A colonial burial ground for African Americans is discovered in New York City.

LIVING HISTORY

Primary sources provide firsthand evidence about a topic. Witnesses to a historical event create primary sources. They include autobiographies, newspaper reports of the time, oral histories, photographs, and memoirs. A secondary source analyzes primary sources, and is one step or more removed from the event. Secondary sources include textbooks, encyclopedias, and commentaries. To view the following primary and secondary sources, go to www.factsfornow.scholastic.com. Enter the keywords **African Americans in the Thirteen Colonies** and look for the Living History logo ⌧.

⌧ **Ads Searching for Runaways** The University of Virginia has many ads for runaway slaves from colonial times online. Visitors to the living museum in Williamsburg also find information on African American life during colonial times, thanks to actors who play people from that era.

⌧ **An African Burial Ground** New York City's African Burial Ground now has a museum run by the National Park Service on the site. The museum shows some of the items found there, and visitors can watch a film about the burial ground.

⌧ **A Bill of Sale** Documents dating back to the early days of the colonies have helped historians understand the details of the colonial slave trade. When selling slaves to each other, owners usually issued documents called bills of sale. These served as legal proof that ownership had been transferred.

⌧ **The Painting of James Armistead** The painting of James Armistead and the man who helped him win his freedom can be seen at the Lafayette College Art Gallery in Easton, Pennsylvania.

RESOURCES

Books

Benoit, Peter. *The Jamestown Colony*. New York: Children's Press, 2012.

Blair, Margaret Whitman. *Liberty or Death: The Surprising Story of Runaway Slaves Who Sided with the British During the American Revolution*. Washington, DC: National Geographic, 2010.

Blashfield, Jean F. *Slavery in America*. New York: Children's Press, 2012.

Collard, Sneed B. *Phillis Wheatley: She Loved Words*. New York: Marshall Cavendish Benchmark, 2010.

Haskins, James, and Kathleen Benson. *Africa: A Look Back*. New York: Marshall Cavendish Benchmark, 2007.

Herr, Melody. *The Slave Trade*. Chicago: Heinemann Library, 2010.

Linde, Barbara M. *Slavery in Early America.* New York: Gareth Stevens Publishing, 2011.

Visit this Scholastic Web site for more information on African Americans in the Thirteen Colonies:
www.factsfornow.scholastic.com
Enter the keywords African Americans in the Thirteen Colonies

GLOSSARY

abolition (a-buh-LIH-shuhn) the official end of something

amended (uh-MEND-id) changed a legal document or a law

ancestors (AN-ses-turz) members of a family who lived long ago

archaeologists (ahr-kee-AH-luh-jists) scientists who study the distant past, often by digging up old buildings, objects, and bones and examining them carefully

bondage (BAHN-dij) the condition of being under the control of someone or something when it is against one's will

discrimination (diss-krim-uh-NAY-shun) unfair treatment of others based on age, race, gender, or other factors

economy (i-KAHN-uh-mee) the system of buying, selling, making things, and managing money in a place

freemen (FREE-men) former slaves who received their freedom

indentured servants (in-DEN-churd SUR-vuhnts) people who agreed to work for someone else for a set number of years, in return for passage to America

Middle Colonies (MID-uhl KAH-luh-neez) a name for New York, Pennsylvania, Delaware, and New Jersey while under English rule

militia (muh-LISH-uh) a group of people who are trained to fight but are not professional soldiers

mulatto (muh-LAH-toh) having a mixture of white and African American family backgrounds

petition (puh-TI-shuhn) a letter signed by many people asking those in power to change their policy or actions

thatched (THACHT) made of dried plants, such as straw or reeds

INDEX

Page numbers in *italics* indicate illustrations.

ABOUT THE AUTHOR

Michael Burgan is the author of more than 250 books for children and young adults, both fiction and nonfiction. His works include books on the Underground Railroad and colonial New York, Maryland, Connecticut, and Massachusetts. His graphic-novel adaptation of *Frankenstein* was a Junior Library Guild selection. A graduate of the University of Connecticut, Burgan is also a produced playwright. He lives in Santa Fe, New Mexico.